Growing Hope

The Therapeutic Benefits of Gardening

Carol Bernardone

Table of Contents

INTRODUCTION 1

CHAPTER 1: HOW IS GARDENING A THERAPEUTIC ACTIVITY? 3

THE THERAPEUTIC WONDERS OF GARDENING.. 4
    Reducing Anxiety 4
    Promoting Emotional Regulation 5
    Sensory Symphony as a Feast for the Senses.. 5
    Calming the Mind and Self-Regulation 6
    Motor Skills Improvement 6
    Enhancing Focus and Dedication 6
    Better Communication Skills... 7
    Building Social Skills.. 7
    Vocational and Life Skill Improvement 7
    Boosting a Sense of Accomplishment and Self-Esteem 8

CHAPTER 2: GARDENING—A POWERFUL THERAPEUTIC TOOL FOR EVERYONE! 9

GARDENING: CONQUERING DISORDERS AND CHALLENGES 9
    Ranging Disabilities 9
    Trauma History and Mental Illness.. 11
    Developmental Disabilities, Intellectual Disabilities, and Limited Mobility . 12
    Autism and Sensory Issues.. 13
    Behavior and Emotional Challenges 14

CHAPTER 3: CASE STUDIES 17

GARDENING AND HEALING 17
    Study #1 17
    Study #2 18
    Study #3 18
REAL STORIES 18

CHAPTER 4: INCORPORATING GARDENING INTO THE EDUCATIONAL AND
THERAPY SETTINGS 23

HOW TO START UP.. 23
    Phase 1: Starting a School or Community Garden................................... 23
    Phase 2: Choosing Appropriate Plants... 24
    Phase 3: Adapting Activities for Different Abilities.................................. 24
    Phase 4: Integrating Garden-Based Learning Into the Curriculum............. 25
    Phase 5: Therapeutic Garden Spaces... 25
SEEDS OF KNOWLEDGE 27

The Benefits of Reading Seed Packets 28

CHAPTER 5: COLLABORATION IS KEY! **31**

WHY COLLABORATION IS IMPORTANT AND HOW IT HELPS 31
The Holistic Approach 31
Comprehensive Understanding 32
Individualized Support 32
Enhanced Program Design 32
Professional Development and Learning 32
SUGGESTIONS FOR FOSTERING EFFECTIVE PARTNERSHIPS 35

CHAPTER 6: POTENTIAL BARRIERS AND CHALLENGES **37**

OVERCOMING CHALLENGES 37
Budget Constraints 37
Limited Space 38
Resistance to Change 40
Lack of Knowledge or Expertise 40
Maintenance and Sustainability 41

CHAPTER 7: USE YOUR RESOURCES **43**

RESOURCES TO USE 43
Websites and Online Resources 43
Books 43
Fun Apps 44

CHAPTER 8: A WELL-ROUNDED APPROACH **47**

TECHNIQUES FOR A WELL-ROUNDED APPROACH 47
Counseling in the Garden 47
Mindfulness Within the Green 47
Social-Emotional Learning 48
Therapeutic Endeavors 48
NURTURING GROWTH AT HOME 49
Step-by-Step Guide on How to Garden at Home 50

CHAPTER 9: GARDENING AND DIVERSITY, EQUITY, AND INCLUSION (DEI) **53**

GARDENING AS AN INCLUSIVE THERAPEUTIC TOOL 53
The Benefits 54

CHAPTER 10: YEAR-ROUND GARDENING **57**

CULTIVATING KNOWLEDGE IN EVERY SEASON 57
Indoor Gardening 57
Selecting Seasonal Plants 58
Alternative Gardening Methods 58
Gardening-Related Arts and Crafts 58

Research *60*

CONCLUSION.. **61**

REFERENCES.. **63**

DEDICATION.. **65**

    A Couple of Takeaways 65

Introduction

Have you ever wondered what a handful of soil could do to unlock your child's potential, regardless of their abilities or challenges? Well, it's time for you to dig deep into this subject because I've spent the last 26 years proving that it can lead to profound possibilities.

I'm Carol Bernardone, a seasoned school-based Occupational Therapist Assistant in Special Education, a Mom and Nana, and the creative force behind a licensed daycare back in the day. But I am more than this; I am going to be your guide on this incredible journey because I am a firm believer in going beyond the average procedure. I want to turn every therapy session into an unforgettable adventure, but not to get too much into my hopes and dreams; let's get into the nitty-gritty of my mission.

Over the years, I have had the opportunity to team up with some amazing people with a similar vision and energy to craft programs that cater to students from the preschool level to high school. I have worked with children with varying disorders, including autism, ODD, ADHD, and many others. And did I mention that, as a mom, I've always had a passion for helping kids grow up to be the best versions of themselves? Well, what exactly do this knowledge and the activities outlined in this book have to do with therapy? To put it simply, I want to turn therapy into something more than the practice kids dread before going in for a session. I want to make it fun with high-interest topics and activities that will light up the child's world. Trust and rapport are my building blocks in this process, and let's not forget the fact that kids are always up for a hands-on and multisensory activity to get their minds off whatever challenges they may face. So, what kind of approach is best? Therapy with gardening! Yep, you read that right!

Well, it's not only going to be about plants but about transforming their little lives. In this book, I am going to spill the beans on real-life stories of kids who went from meh to wow! All of this was thanks to a little bit of time with the soil and seeds. And hey, I know my focus has been mostly on kids my entire life, but guess what? These gardening principles will work for everyone, not just the little ones or the not-so-little ones. It's great for adults as well. When it comes to stress reduction, personal growth, cognitive stimulation, and more, the garden has it all figured out. Think of it as a therapy session that comes in all shapes and sizes and is tailored to suit your needs.

Gardening isn't just for those with a spacious front or backyard. It is a lifeline, a tool that can help support kids facing all sorts of challenges. From emotional trauma to physical disabilities and everything in between, the garden becomes a haven, a place where scents soothe, colors pop, and nature's touch is a balm for not only the mind but the soul as well. This is the place where they will get to discover who they are and connect with the world around them, all while building resilience. This isn't just about what goes on in the therapy room; it's about adapting activities, practical strategies, and some garden magic that all fit into the curriculum. Sound intriguing? Well, it's possible. With collaboration, everyone can come together to create a space where every kid thrives. So whether you're in a community space, a school, or just chilling at home, therapeutic gardening is a year-round ticket that you can use to unlock the incredible potential in every child.

Get ready to embark on a journey of growth, resilience, and a lot of green magic. Let's make therapeutic gardening more than just a concept, but a way of life.

Chapter 1:

How Is Gardening a Therapeutic Activity?

Let's enter the garden area, where the soil becomes a canvas of seeds for you to transform into whispers of potential and possibility. Before we get started with all the fascinating information that comes from soil, seeds, and tending to the earth, let's first clarify one little detail. Gardening, in essence, isn't about having a large piece of land to grow immeasurable plants, herbs, and fruit. No, it can be as simple as indoor planting using small gardening pots, raised beds, hanging gardens, window boxes, or windowsill gardening. All that matters here is that you are planting and eventually, every leaf will tell a story of growth. This is how I feel whenever I see the beauty of the sunflowers I grow every year—my favorite flowers.

In this chapter, we're going to look at the enchanted world of therapeutic gardening, where the power of nature is going to intertwine with the resilience and potential of young hearts. So, let's get ready to explore why gardening isn't just a pastime but a therapeutic symphony that is going to give children the source of growth, confidence, and resilience needed to become capable individuals.

The Therapeutic Wonders of Gardening

Therapy isn't only about a therapist sitting at a desk and the affected person lying down on the couch and talking throughout the hour-long session. There are techniques and activities that have come to light that show that the mind and body can be healed and rejuvenated using other means. Gardening is one approach that serves as a therapeutic and inclusive activity. It offers more than just a handful of benefits to children of all ages, regardless of the challenges they face. Because of its multisensory nature and inherent qualities, the garden is a safe and nurturing environment that will support children while enhancing their emotional healing, cognitive development, sensory integration, and overall well-being. Let's look at a few ways in which gardening is therapeutic and more than a hobby (Barnett, 2021).

Reducing Anxiety

Imagine a world where stress can take the back seat and tranquility becomes the norm. Gardening can do just that. By tending to plants and feeling the earth beneath your fingers while immersing yourself in nature, these activities come together to act as a potent stress-buster.

The rhythmic dance of weeding and watering will become a lulling symphony for your child's mind. Just by sitting there, looking, and breathing in the goodness of nature, stress-reducing hormones are released, thus ushering in a sense of calm and peace from deep within.

Promoting Emotional Regulation

Gardening is an activity that allows children to bond with nature.

Consistent participation in gardening activities becomes a very powerful tool for emotional regulation, since nurturing plants fosters stability. It also provides children with a healthy outlet to process and express their feelings. Imagine children playing with soil, digging deep into the ground and covering up the seeds, waiting for them to grow. They learn to channel their emotions in a positive light as they grow and care for plants.

Sensory Symphony as a Feast for the Senses

Gardening is a sensory extravaganza for anyone. When it comes to the texture of flowers, leaves, and soil, the symphony of the scents from the plants, the chorus of the insects and birds, and the vibrant hues of all of the flowers and crops, all of these contribute to that sensory feast. For children who have sensory processing challenges, the garden becomes a playful environment to develop their exploration. They will engage and integrate their senses in this natural and therapeutic setting.

Here is a picture of my granddaughter and I indulging in some gardening.

Calming the Mind and Self-Regulation

Over the years, with recent studies in therapeutical activities like meditation and yoga, we have discovered that nature has a way of calming a storm within (Robbins, 2020). Many people who use natural settings as the backdrop for their therapy sessions tend to experience a gentle guide into relaxation and self-regulation. With gardening, the activities encourage mindfulness. This helps children manage their anxiety, cope with stress, find peace, and conquer their agitated thoughts. The movements of watering and weeding are rhythmic and become a source of comfort for their young minds.

Motor Skills Improvement

To care for the garden, kids need to use their hands and minds. From finger dexterity to hand-eye coordination, planting and caring for plants will tune their fine motor skills. Let's not forget the digging, working, and handling of garden tools, which also come together to contribute toward the growth of robust gross motor skills.

Enhancing Focus and Dedication

The world is a noisy place and there's always something trying to grab your attention.

With gardening, it becomes the focal point whenever a child commits to the activity. The structured and engaging nature of the tasks will capture their attention while encouraging sustained focus. This is a hands-on experience that helps children stay attentive to something that is fun and yet educational and therapeutic. It fosters improved focus and attention span, which is especially beneficial for those with attention difficulties.

Better Communication Skills

Since this is a therapeutic activity, gardening won't be silent work. Children are curious creatures and you will have the opportunity to discuss plants, how the growth cycle works, procedures for caring for the plants, terms related to gardening, and so much more to ease the curiosity and equip them with the necessary knowledge for gardening successfully. With garden-related conversations, you will discover a vibrant way to nurture children's communication skills as they get to describe their experiences and share their observations amidst the greenery.

Building Social Skills

Gardening is more than plants growing; it's about children growing socially as well. This activity is going to consist of collaboration efforts between peers, siblings, or adults as opportunities for teamwork, turn-taking, and joint problem-solving arise. Remember, the garden is a non-intimidating stage where children can express and discuss their feelings and experiences comfortably. Be there to support them and assist them in this journey.

Vocational and Life Skill Improvement

Look beyond the plants and soil; gardens can become classrooms as well. With this activity, valuable vocational and life skills are developed as they learn the ins and outs of plant cultivation, master horticultural practices, and take charge of garden maintenance, which contributes toward their vocational training.

The skills developed do extend beyond the garden gates as they shape their practical abilities, which can be used in various contexts.

Boosting a Sense of Accomplishment and Self-Esteem

In the garden, effort will eventually pay off. As children witness the positive moments—plants growing, flowers blooming, or vegetables flourishing—it will become a tangible source of pride for them. With the constant need to navigate challenges, success and gardening will become mirrors for them, reflecting their capabilities. It will become a pathway to a system for building a positive self-image while nurturing a sense of accomplishment.

In conclusion, it's important that you remember one important fact: This isn't just a hobby; it is a journey that will pave the way for emotional healing, sensory integration, and cognitive development for our little ones. But hold on tight; the garden's secrets are far from over. In the chapters to come, we are going to unearth more wonders, cultivate wisdom, and witness the garden in full bloom. Until then, let the seeds planted today grow with promises of blooming tomorrow.

Chapter 2:

Gardening—A Powerful Therapeutic Tool for Everyone!

Let's step into the world of therapeutic gardening, which expands to welcome every child looking for a haven. Remember that the soil we tread upon is a canvas for growth in this journey. It becomes a sanctuary where disabilities and challenges become possibilities.

Gardening: Conquering Disorders and Challenges

Let's get into the nitty-gritty of how gardening can help every child move forward from their mental health and behavioral challenges (Ainamani et al., 2022).

Ranging Disabilities

Attention-Deficit/Hyperactivity Disorder (ADHD)

With this disorder, kids can't focus for long. When gardening, the work isn't boring or set on repeat. The daily activities hold a different sort of intrigue. Kids will want to immerse themselves in them. From there, constant practice naturally enhances focus and attention.

Also, this is a multi-sensory and hands-on experience. It's a calming activity that offers structure while promoting self-regulation.

Sensory Processing Disorder (SPD)

Moving on, the garden is going to become a sensory symphony as every texture, scent, sound, and color becomes a note in the unique melody.

It's a therapeutic journey that guides children through the world of sensory stimuli that help them regulate responses effectively. They are safe to explore, touch, and feel, allowing them to get accustomed to new sensations.

Developmental Delays

Going through the motions of planting, watering, and harvesting is a stepping stone for fine motor skills, grip strength, hand-eye coordination, vocabulary, and so on. The garden is going to serve as a hands-on classroom that transforms abstract concepts into tangible lessons. There will be a convergence between math, language, science, and environmental awareness. They will see the world differently, which will help them grow.

Physical Disabilities

Facing challenges due to a disability or limitation can evoke feelings of vulnerability.

With gardening, no child is left behind. The techniques are adaptive and accessible to all. This creates a path of inclusivity for those with physical disabilities. For example, vertical gardens, raised beds, and container gardening will open doors for those with limited mobility or strength. The bottom line is that every child can grow a garden.

Emotional and Behavioral Disorders

Emotional troubles can be quite turbulent, but it is possible to find solace in the embrace of the garden. Those with emotional and behavioral disorders discover a therapeutic haven where they get to nurture a sense of calm and decrease stress levels. It becomes a vessel for improving and enhancing their self-esteem, emotional regulation, and coping skills.

Trauma History and Mental Illness

No one expects a child to go through difficult times. However, some of them do experience harsh realities and conditions that evoke trauma and, at times, mental illness. Let's look at a few ways in which gardening can support the healing and well-being of such children.

- It provides a sense of control, as children will be able to make decisions as well as become more resilient as they get to nurture plant life. When a child experiences trauma or a mental illness, their empowerment and independence decline. Gardening helps them regain that sense of empowerment.

- They learn to embrace the present moment, as the processes become a tool for grounding and mindfulness. Their senses entwine with the natural world and this will guide them toward that state of mindful immersion.

- When children focus and use their hands to tend to the soil and complete all of the gardening tasks, their emotions simmer down as they learn how to calm their minds through emotional regulation.

- Experiencing the growth, positivity, and setbacks, gardening mirrors the personal struggles and victories that these children face. It becomes a symbol that fosters conversation about resilience, healing, and growth.

- With the embrace of community guidance or therapeutic programs, gardening will become a social affair. It will reduce their feelings of isolation while fostering a sense of belonging.

- Gardening can be a conduit for therapeutic benefits like stress management, elevation of mood, overall enhancing one's emotional well-being. It provides a holistic experience that will transcend the boundaries of trauma and mental health challenges for affected children.

- Witnessing the growth and beauty of plants coming to life will provide children with a sense of self-worth. Knowing that they are capable of doing something positive can help boost their low sense of self-worth by reinforcing self-esteem.

The garden provides adaptability and a healing touch. It emerges as a safe haven for children navigating the realm of traumatic history and mental wellness.

Now, let's move on to the next issue.

Developmental Disabilities, Intellectual Disabilities, and Limited Mobility

Gardening can also become a valuable activity for children who have certain conditions that limit their mobility and affect their cognitive and physical development.

- Firstly, children get to touch the soil, feel the leaves, smell the scent of the flowers, and listen to the sounds of nature like chirping insects and buzzing bees. This is like a sensory adventure.

- The activities are like a brain workout where children get to figure out how to care for the plants, pick the ones they want to grow, and organize their tools.

- The repetitive movements help children stay relaxed, focused, grounded, and happier. Think of it as a happiness booster.

- Regardless of how big or small a task, there's always something to do.

- There will be certain tasks that the kids will need to do together, which will encourage talking, sharing, and working as a team.

- Taking care of plants and ensuring that they are tended to daily teaches children how to be responsible.

- Gardening is adaptable, as we have already mentioned. Tools and spaces can be adapted as needed.

- The skills that the children learn will improve other parts of their lives. Not only are they learning to care for plants, but they are also developing life skills such as responsibility, caring for and nurturing others, and actively using their decision-making skills to reach their goals more effectively.

So, allow the kids to grab their gardening tools and adapt as needed. They will grow together, their well-being will improve, new skills will develop, and a sense of accomplishment will be achieved.

Now, let's discuss the next issue.

Autism and Sensory Issues

Gardening is quite beneficial, as it can help with disorders that are difficult to navigate or understand. Let's get into how it can help with autism and sensory issues in more detail.

- With gardening, children will get to touch different textures and smell different scents. They listen to different sounds of nature and see bursts of colors. This will improve how their senses work together.

- Doing repetitive movements is calming and acts as a natural stress-buster. It's like receiving a calming hug from nature.

- With constant thoughts revolving around solving issues, planning certain tasks, and achieving certain goals for the garden, it serves as a brain workout.

- Gardening can include others. So, children will develop social bonds and make friendships.

- Finally, there is the benefit that gardening doesn't have to fit a specific route. It is a custom adventure that is designed for any child.

The bottom line is that gardening is more than just digging in the dirt and planting a seed; it is a journey that will bring about skilled achievement, connection, and relaxation.

Behavior and Emotional Challenges

Given the above benefits, it is only natural that gardening would be able to assist children in regulating their emotions.

- Kids will be able to express their feelings in a positive way, as the tasks help them manage their anxiety and stress levels.

- They work on controlling their impulsive behavior. With gardening, they learn to follow through, take ownership of their actions, and understand that neglect of responsibility has consequences.

- This will bring about a sense of accomplishment and self-worth. The motions of tending a garden sow confidence.

- Kids will see the fruits of their labor, from growth and blooming to harvest. They get to discover their own capabilities.

The bottom line is that gardening can create a supportive environment for children facing various challenges. It's like adding a splash of nature to traditional strategies to create a program that will support their unique journey. This isn't just about the green, but gardening will also foster a sense of connection, accomplishment, and well-being. In the next chapter, we're going to dive into some key strategies to prove the fact that gardening has the potential to assist our kids and help them become the best adults they can be.

Chapter 3:

Case Studies

Now, there's no use suggesting therapy from gardening without some research to back it up. After all, no method is guaranteed without some research having been done to prove that it does work. Let's look at some case studies and a couple of personal stories of how gardening helps improve the lives of children who face various challenges.

Gardening and Healing

Suzanne L. Kohlmeyer researched the health effects of gardens and healthcare settings as well as what aspects or benefits therapeutic gardening would offer children (Kohlmeyer, 2006). She found that therapeutic gardens offer healing potential to children, helping them restore their health and well-being. From her research, it is clear that healing gardens tailored for children have an impact on their development. Children always want to play, as this is a medium for them to work through internal conflict, express their fears, and communicate their desires nonverbally.

Study #1

From her research, there is one healing space in Berkeley and Boston—an urban oasis in an elementary school.

The school replaced asphalt with running water, land, and plants. The impact of this change was that the natural scenery and garden activities led to positive changes in the children's social behavior and boosted their self-confidence. The garden eventually became a space where the children had a chance to control their environment, which fostered a sense of identity and belonging (Kohlmeyer, 2006).

Study #2

In Boston, Massachusetts, a children's hospital opened up a therapeutic garden in 1956. It boasted a half-acre rectangular garden. It was enclosed by a hospital building, which provided a sense of safety in the urban oasis. There were sculptures, water features, and vibrant plant life that created an enjoyable refuge for the children and their siblings, parents, relatives, and hospital staff. This study went on to prove that it didn't only benefit the children but everyone who visited. They enjoyed the sense of peace and calm that the natural setting provided (Kohlmeyer, 2006).

Study #3

This study by Frontiers showed that there was a difference between children who spent more time in the classroom and those who spent time outdoors. School gardens, especially in primary schools, have been used to develop children's cognitive and emotional abilities. The study was done on 53 children, both girls and boys, aged between 11 and 12 years old. Those who spent time in the school garden showed more socially competent behavior compared to those who only spent their time in the classroom. These children were happier, showed pride in themselves, and were more surprised and full of wonder than the others, who showed more fear or anxiety as well as disgust in the classroom (Pollin & Retzlaff-Fürst, 2021).

Real Stories

Here are two of my personal experiences regarding gardening with children and how it helped them thrive.

Jack is a former student of mine who is a true-life example of how gardening helps therapeutically. Jack struggled with reading and writing, emotional regulation, and attention. But Jack loved to work. He loved to dig, plant, rake, shovel, and so on. Jack is a very hard and conscientious worker with a vision beyond his years.

Initially, Jack didn't want to come to therapy to work on writing, self-regulation, or other areas he struggled with. Knowing Jack and many other kids like him, I needed to gain his trust before he would want to engage in any academic tasks. Using gardening as a segue, Jack began to trust me as his Occupational Therapist. Jack and I planned Earth Day activities that led to him making lists of things that could be done to improve the school grounds—I would sneak in printing or keyboarding skills wherever I could! We edited his lists, typed them up, and shared them with the school principal. (i.e., addressing technology skills, executive functioning, etc.) Jack participated in and organized many planting and gardening activities at school, which built his self-esteem and reduced stress and anxiety. Jack eventually looked forward to therapy sessions and would often ask to come during free time to work on gardening projects or to simply work on cleaning up and beautifying the school grounds. Building a relationship around Jack's love of nature and gardening allowed me to address many academic, social-emotional, and self-regulation goals with Jack.

Before returning to his district school, Jack wanted to build his own garden. With help from Gary, our school's Director of Buildings and Grounds at the time, Jack made his garden a reality.

Here is a before and after picture of Jack's garden. He drew it out, weeded and rototilled it, made a list of items we needed, and asked for resources and help as needed. Jack even added a drainage system, weed cover, mulch, and a rock barrier. Jack has continued to use his skills and love of gardening to help his neighbors, friends, and family. He plans to open his own landscaping business someday. There is no doubt in my mind that Jack will make this and many other dreams come true!

Corey, another one of my students, went on to say that planting makes him feel happy and calm. In the pictures below, you can see how a little garden magic helped grow the watermelon in his hands. Notice the grass planters on the window sill behind Corey. Another one of the many indoor planting experiences we enjoyed!

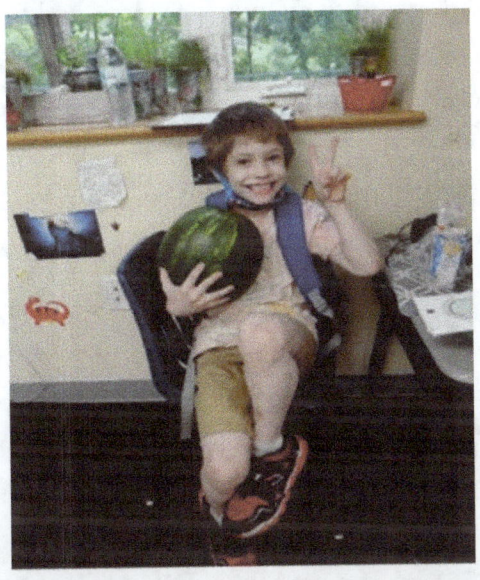

Corey came to me as an Occupational Therapy student with goals to address his fine motor skills, printing skills, and emotional regulation. Corey knew he struggled in these areas and did not want to participate in therapy. At first, he even refused to attend sessions. Enticing Corey with some in-class planting and nature craft activities led to some outside garden related activities. As Corey's confidence grew, he became more willing to write and draw pictures of his gardening experiences, thus addressing his Individualized Education Plan goals. Corey now looks forward to attending sessions and has made amazing gains overall.

From these, we can now recognize that thoughtfully designed healing gardens that promote spending time in nature can positively impact the well-being of children. It provides them with a nurturing space for growth, play, and recovery.

Chapter 4:

Incorporating Gardening Into the Educational and Therapy Settings

Many like to say that nature is the best teacher, and when it comes to the world of education and therapy, let's be honest—from what we have seen, gardens can become transformative classrooms on their own. Let's move on to the process of initiating a school or community garden while garnering support from administrators, parents, and community members to set the stage for success. Remember that the future lies in our children, and only by ensuring that they are given all of the tools to become strong, independent, confident, and skilled individuals can we call ourselves successful teachers and leaders. Let's look at how we can incorporate gardening into everyday life for our kids.

How to Start Up

Let's look at a detailed guide on how you can initiate and implement a garden for therapy in an educational setting.

Phase 1: Starting a School or Community Garden

- Step 1: Engage with the school administration, parents, and community members to build a strong support network.

- Step 2: Evaluate the potential and possible locations for the garden. Look for fertile ground with sunlight exposure, accessibility, and safety considerations in place.

- Step 3: Obtain the necessary resources, which include gardening tools, compost, seeds, or plants, through donations or partnerships with garden centers or local nurseries. Keep in mind that you might be able to obtain funds via grants and other related programs.

- Step 4: Come up with a comprehensive schedule for watering, weeding, and general upkeep. This entire process can involve students, teachers, and volunteers to share the responsibilities to ensure that the garden is sustained.

Phase 2: Choosing Appropriate Plants

- Step 1: Consider your local climate and the seasons. For example, you can't plant plants that bloom in the warmer months during the autumn and winter seasons. The plants should also suit the school year since they won't be tended to during school closures.

- Step 2: Investigate thoroughly before selecting the plants. Choose a variety of plants that will be a boon to the sensory experience for the children. Try colorful flowers, aromatic herbs, and textured foliage.

- Step 3: Encourage plant groups from a diverse range. Go the extra mile to teach kids the importance of biodiversity and the interconnectedness between plant life and ecosystems.

Phase 3: Adapting Activities for Different Abilities

- Step 1: Since every child is different, you'll have to provide accessible tools for all of them. Utilize the tools with ergonomic handles or adjustable heights to accommodate children with physical challenges.

- Step 2: Analyze each task and then modify it based on each child's ability. For those with specific challenges, be creative and modify the activity as needed. You can also assign responsibilities according to each age group.

- Step 3: Incorporate tactile and olfactory items such as textured plants, aromatic herbs, or materials to offer a wide variety of sensory options.

Phase 4: Integrating Garden-Based Learning Into the Curriculum

- Step 1: Find ways to incorporate gardening into different subjects. For example, in science, they get to study plant life cycles, or in math, they get to measure plant growth. It can also be incorporated in language arts as they write about their gardening experiences. In art class, they can create garden-inspired artwork.

- Step 2: Encourage the students to ask questions, explore scientific concepts through hands-on garden experiences, and conduct experiments. Try to give them the freedom to explore what they want in the garden. This way, their curiosity is satisfied and their questions are answered.

- Step 3: Incorporate some reflective activities to help the students document their observations. For example, you could encourage them to keep garden journals where they write down and reflect on their experiences and make connections between their gardening experiences and personal growth.

Phase 5: Therapeutic Garden Spaces

- Step 1: Create sensory areas by designating sections in the garden that will incorporate different sensory elements, like windchimes, fragrant and colorful flowers, textured surfaces, and comfortable seating for some sensory experiences and deep relaxation.

- Step 2: Integrate mindful practices or activities into the garden like guided meditations, breathing exercises, and others, which will all promote emotional well-being and self-awareness for children.

- Step 3: Develop specific projects that will align with therapeutic activities. Allow them to bond with nature as much as possible.

The bottom line is, as you implement these strategies, you can successfully incorporate gardening into an educational setting or some of your therapy sessions. It will not only provide students with valuable hands-on experiences but also opportunities for growth, learning, and other therapeutic benefits.

This is Mary, a Speech-Language Pathologist who I had the pleasure of working with for a few years. Many considered us the best SPOT (Speech & Occupational Therapy) team ever! We incorporated gardening activities into many of our co-treatments, benefiting my Occupational Therapy and her Speech Therapy students.

Seeds of Knowledge

Moving on to a bit of reading, this is where we unveil the secrets on the back of seed packets. Every packet holds a key to a fun and educational adventure. It may sound a bit goofy, but picture this from a child's point of view. The information on the back of the seed package isn't just about planting the seeds. It spreads knowledge in the most delightful way. Children are curious creatures and ask a lot of questions. I'm continuously astonished at how much information they absorb when they are enjoying such hands-on activities. By sharing with them the information on the back of a seed package, they will see how simple seeds can hold powerful and great potential, much like themselves. So, let's get into an activity that can become a game-changer, making learning come to life.

The Benefits of Reading Seed Packets

- First, they dive into the world of words. Reading new information is like a literacy fiesta where children can get to decode words, build vocabulary, and understand how the world of planting and gardening works. They get to indulge in the literacy of a flourishing garden.

- It's a scientific adventure on its own. It divulges secrets about plants, showing their scientific name, what they need to grow, and their daily needs until and after germination. Think of it as a treasure trove of information that makes gardening like a problem-solving quiz.

- There will be fun math puzzles to solve. Children will need to figure out how deep to plant a seed and how much water is needed each day, and there are certain calculations to be made, from planting distances to seed count. This journey will also nurture a garden of math skills in which children will need to calculate, estimate, and make comparisons.

- Let's not forget about the geography lessons. Seed packets give information on planting times in relation to regional areas. It is a global adventure and kids get to explore the world of horticulture, where they discover the ABCs of agriculture, all from the comfort of their garden or classroom.

- Environmental awareness blooms as kids get to learn from seed packets the tales of plant origins, climate protection, and the ecological impact of plants. They will get to dive into the building side of gardening as they learn not just about biodiversity but also how to improve on their skills and become sustainability champions.

- Finally, there are the writing and communication advantages, where kids get to draw and write about their experiences. Remember that the seed packet isn't just a source of information; it inspires creativity as well. The children will get to write down notes, record observations, and even create their own labels for the plants. It's a storytelling adventure, but with a little green magic!

So, there you have it! Gardening as a form of therapy goes even beyond the soil. Something as simple as the packaging of the seeds can be useful. There's always some benefit that the children can receive from this activity and it all revolves around how you use it.

As we come to the close of this enchanting chapter, it's time to get ready to imagine the joy of working together, planting seeds of friendship, and tilling the garden of endless possibilities for our future—the children.

Chapter 5:

Collaboration Is Key!

Let's step back for a second and imagine a vibrant, green, and thriving garden with the laughter of children, the rustling of leaves, and the shared joy of everyone coming together to learn. Imagine that the magic doesn't just happen with a single person but with a collaborative dance of therapists, educators, and garden experts. This is the exciting chapter where we get to look into collaboration, where every hand is going to come forward, bringing a unique touch to cultivate a garden of possibilities. It's time to unravel the secrets of working together and how it will unlock the potential of gardening for children facing a variety of challenges.

Why Collaboration Is Important and How it Helps

Have you ever heard the phrase, "Alone, we are weak, but together, we are stronger than ever? This statement is true even in therapy and gardening.

The Holistic Approach

When we come together as educators, therapists, and garden experts to work toward one goal, we are giving the children a holistic approach that isn't just about classes, therapy sessions, or seeds, but nurturing the whole child. Why is this so? Well, think of it: We are going to bring about therapeutic, educational, and horticultural magic, which is going to create a garden that caters to every side of the square. Each one of these professionals is going to come in with their own set of skills and knowledge and mix them all up to create an approach that is going to be beneficial to a child's overall well-being.

Comprehensive Understanding

Let's have a little fun and picture the coming together of superheroes, like that assembling scene in the Avengers movie. Each individual has their own superpower. Now, when it comes to educators who wield the knowledge of academic curriculum, therapists to carry the emotional intelligence shields, and garden experts to swing that horticultural hammer, together they all form a powerhouse of understanding on how they can integrate gardening seamlessly into education and therapy. This will make it a very comprehensive experience for the children. Not to sound too geeky, but I hope that made sense.

Individualized Support

Let's get personal. When we collaborate, this isn't just a team huddle. This is where the tailoring activities for each student starts. We get to share what we know and use our knowledge to come up with roles that are based on the unique strengths of each child. This way, they get to have a garden suited to their needs and abilities.

Enhanced Program Design

Let's get to design thinking: Everyone comes together to ensure that every facet is covered through gardening, education, and therapy. So, what exactly is the result of all of this? Well, it's going to be an enhanced program that is designed not just to be effective but to be downright innovative. Can you picture the awesomeness?

Professional Development and Learning

The development and learning don't just start with the children; educators will also be able to learn to tell the difference between a tulip and a daffodil; a therapist will be able to pick up new tips on therapeutic gardening; and garden experts will become pros at understanding the unique needs of children and students with varying abilities. This is going to serve as a mutual exchange of knowledge that will make both adults and children a bit greener and a whole lot wiser.

In therapeutic gardening, collaboration is key because every voice matters and every perspective counts. This journey is about helping children flourish in their lives but with teamwork, we get to turn their learning experiences into a flourishing garden of endless possibilities. I would like to share something that Gary, our Building and Grounds Supervisor who made incredible connections with many of our students, especially Jack, said, "Having the opportunity to work with Jack and several other students was extremely rewarding. In traditional settings, a maintenance supervisor most likely wouldn't be invited to be as involved as I was able to be, and I'm very grateful for the experience. I would love to see this happen more in other settings as well. It was so neat to see how some students were more willing to get their classwork done so they could participate in planting or related activities. It really motivated them and made a huge difference in their behavior and overall well-being. I especially enjoyed working with Jack and helping him make his garden a reality."

I've had the pleasure of collaborating with amazing people like Gary and Peter, who share the same vision and energy.

Peter said, "I didn't believe I could really reach our students until I had the chance to work shoulder-to-shoulder, one-on-one with them in a garden. These opportunities allow me the time to help unpack the invisible backpacks they were carrying, which contained their short-lived experiences. We had talks about parents and grandparents who also shared with them their experiences and knowledge. I've been blessed with the chance to work with our students to build our garden from the ground up (no pun intended!). Sharing my experiences and knowledge that I've obtained through myriad gardening creations and expansions has been more than gratifying when those students who we've passed onto our high school want to return to the middle school and work again with the teachers they feel connected to. In closing, it's difficult to imagine a more rewarding and satisfying vocation than teaching that allows us these opportunities."

The takeaway is that, no matter who you are or what you do, by coming together to move forward and assist our children with healing and progress, we can make a difference.

Now, let's move on to how you can make this journey work seamlessly.

Suggestions for Fostering Effective Partnerships

Partnership is almost always the backbone of turning any dream into a reality, especially when it comes to situations where more than one person is involved. In this case, when it comes to children facing challenges, we need to work together to ensure that they have the best chance at moving forward. So, buckle up as we get ready to explore the art of collaboration in crafting impactful programs.

- Open communication is the secret ingredient of effective partnerships, ensuring that people can work together without issues popping up and dividing them. Encourage each other to share your gardening hacks and secret fertilizers!

- You will need to identify the strengths of each team member and discover what they will bring to the table. This is the essence of an effective partnership—assigning roles to make the most of each person's capabilities. Think of it as creating a superhero squad where each person plays a vital role.

- You will also need to establish shared objectives and goals so that everyone is on the same page. Make sure that these goals align with education, horticulture, and therapy. This will become the guiding compass for your decisions, plans, and evaluations to ensure that everyone is moving in the same direction.

- Before jumping into things, everyone will need a bit of training. Also encourage continuous learning through conferences, certifications, and workshops. Educators, therapists, and garden experts will have to become ever-evolving gardeners as they enrich their understanding of the intricate dance between your goals and objectives. Keep in mind that the aim here is to help children with learning, physical, social-emotional and developmental challenges. We want to help them overcome their difficulties, expand their abilities, and achieve their goals. This won't be an easy process; it will take time, effort, education, and dedication.

- Effective partnerships involve regular reflection and evaluation to make sure you're effectively working toward your goals, so as a team, you will need to share your observations, feedback, and notes on collaborative efforts. From your analysis and any new information discovered between planning sessions, ensure that the program is a dynamic space that is perfectly tailored to the evolving needs of the students.

By implementing the above strategies, you will be able to obtain effective partnerships with like-minded people who are striving toward achieving the same goal. With effective communication and a driving force behind each of you, this process of using a garden as a therapeutic process for these children will become seamless.

Now that we have covered the secret of collaboration and effective partnerships, it's time to get ready for the next adventure, where you learn how to navigate the maze of potential barriers and challenges. But worry not, because every challenge is a seed waiting to sprout into an opportunity. Let's move forward and discover how we can make every child's gardening experience truly transformative.

Chapter 6:

Potential Barriers and Challenges

The garden is full of promise and every seed planted has the potential to bloom into a vibrant plant. To be honest, the journey isn't simple. It's like going through a maze with a narrow path that can hinder the growth of budding plants.

In our exploration of gardening for children as a form of therapy, it's time for us to navigate through the labyrinth of potential barriers and challenges that could come up to stand between the growth and the transformative power of gardening.

Educational settings serve as a crucial canvas for the minds and hearts of children. We have already looked at the immense potential of gardens as therapeutic spaces for growth and learning. Now, let's get into the shadows that could cast some doubt on the seamless integration of gardening programs. Let's get into how you can overcome these challenges and continue in your quest to create an enriching environment for these children.

Overcoming Challenges

It is inevitable not to find at least one challenge that will pop up whenever you are starting a new process or going through a challenging but beneficial situation. Some of the potential barriers or challenges that you can expect to face include the following, but we will look beyond the difficulty and see just how exactly you can overcome them:.

Budget Constraints

Tight budgets can be quite a challenge because they can limit the resources that are allocated to gardening programs. The disadvantage of this is that it hinders the purchase of necessary tools, seeds, maintenance supplies and so on. Without a budget, it can be very difficult to secure the setup of a gardening system.

To overcome this issue:

- You will need to forge partnerships with local businesses, nurseries, or community groups. Try to find out whether they can donate resources or offer discounts on certain items.

- You could also post flyers or put up posters on notification boards in the community centers to bring awareness to what you are trying to do and then garner support from the locals.

- You can do some research and explore grants or funding opportunities that are specifically designed for educational or therapeutic gardening initiatives. You may be surprised at how many programs you'll discover when you start digging for them!

Limited Space

Since this is mainly an outdoor activity, insufficient space will restrict the creation of expressive gardens. It will also limit the scope and variety of the plants that can be included. This will also cause a problem with what type of sensory items or plants you can bring in, as some of them need large spaces to grow and thrive. If plants are squashed together, they are less likely to flourish.

To overcome this:

- Try out vertical gardening, where you use walls, pots, or hanging planters to make the most out of little space similar to this picture of my nephew, proud of his container cucumbers.

- Practice container gardening, which allows for flexibility and adaptability in various settings. This allows gardening inside classrooms or small outdoor areas. It will also save on the budget, as it makes it easier to use recyclable objects to use as planters.

Resistance to Change

Some of us can be set in our ways, and there will be resistance from administrators, educators, or parents who are skeptical about integrating gardening into the curriculum or therapeutic programs. After all, many don't trust new processes easily because they have no knowledge about them.

To overcome this,

- you can conduct workshops and presentations to highlight the benefits of gardening for children.

- try to address concerns and showcase success stories to bring awareness to those who are skeptical.

- initiate a small-scale pilot program to demonstrate the positive outcomes before you go into full-scale implementation. This will gradually win over those skeptics.

Lack of Knowledge or Expertise

Similar to the point above, inadequate understanding of gardening practices, especially when it comes to educators, therapists, or school staff, may not want to implement such a process. They might feel that it could be a waste of time or too expensive.

To overcome this,

- provide workshops and training sessions on gardening techniques, plant care, and programming implementation.

- collaborate with some experts to offer guidance or even direct involvement for those who aren't knowledgeable on the subject.

Maintenance and Sustainability

With concerns about the ongoing demands of the garden, it could deter initiation or pose challenges in sustaining the program.

To overcome this,

- involve students, staff, and volunteers. This will ensure that there is a shared responsibility.

- integrate gardening into the curriculum. This will make it a part of the students responsibilities and will foster a sense of ownership and commitment as well.

It's true that some of these barriers may cast long shadows, but looking at them in a positive light, they are an opportunity for creative problem-solving and resilience. Understanding that these challenges could pop up, you will be able to employ innovative solutions that will transform the constraints into stepping stones. In the next chapter, we're going to explore the art of resource utilization, where you get to discover how you can make the most of what is available to create a vibrant and sustainable gardening program.

Chapter 7:

Use Your Resources

This chapter is a little different. We won't go too deep into the details about specific information, but it's time for us to enrich your knowledge and help you find inspiration for your gardening programs with specific books, apps, and websites. So, get ready to dive into tools that offer new ideas.

Resources to Use

Websites and Online Resources

You can visit the following sites for more information to assist you in the gardening-for-therapy journey (Mitchell, n.d.).

- KidsGardening.org

- Edible School Yard Project

- National Garden Associations Kids Gardening

- School Garden Wizard

- Got Dirt?

- Nutrients for Life Foundation

Books

The following books have information on how you can begin a therapeutic garden, learn how to design it, and implement certain techniques and strategies to ensure that the children are receiving the best gardening and therapeutic program that you can offer.

- *Gardening Lab for Kids* by Renata Fossen Brown

- *Gardening - Science - The School Garden Curriculum* by Kaci Rae Christopher

- *How to Garden and Grow: Gardening as Therapy for Children with SEND* by Becky Pinniger

- *Gardening for Children with Autism Spectrum Disorders and Special Educational Needs: Engaging with Nature to Combat Anxiety, Promote Sensory Integration, and Build Social Skills* by Natasha Etherington

- *School and Garden: A Complete Guide for Parent and Teachers* by Arden Bucklin-Sporer and Rachel Kathleen Pringle

Fun Apps

The apps listed below will help with identifying plants, pests, and diseases. They also give you the ability to interact with lessons on planting, nurturing, and harvesting, which make gardening fun and accessible. You get to take photos of leaves and an app will help you identify the species. There are other fun apps you can explore in your preferred app store. You can use specific keywords like "apps to assist with gardening" or "gardening apps for kids" or "apps to identify plant and insect species."

- Garden Compass

- KidzGrow

- My Garden: The RHS App

- YardMap

- Leafsnap

These apps are going to bring an element of playfulness to the learning experience, which will foster curiosity and engagement in the world. Incorporate these resources into your program for a guaranteed educational adventure.

As we come to the end of the chapter, note that there are countless resources out there that will help with your program. These resources will offer you a wealth of knowledge and support.

Now, moving forward, we are going to look at the essence of a well-rounded approach to gardening education. We will look at a few strategies that you could choose to seamlessly integrate various elements to ensure that your gardening program is not only academic but also offers a holistic approach for the growth and well-being of the children.

Chapter 8:

A Well-Rounded Approach

In the symphony of therapeutic and educational gardening, coming up with a well-rounded approach is similar to composing a masterpiece. As you move forward in this journey, it's time for us to look into the transformative power of a comprehensive strategy and techniques that go beyond the soil and seeds to cultivate resilient and thriving individuals.

Techniques for a Well-Rounded Approach

Counseling in the Garden

The garden can become a counseling environment where nature becomes therapeutic. You can create designated areas that represent various emotions, discuss them, and explain that all feeling are o.k. and that it's a safe place to express them. To do this, you can plant seeds that symbolize joy, resilience, or even moments of challenge. You could even link areas of the garden with whatever Social Emotional Curriculum your school or community practices. As the metaphorical emotions grow, conversations can blossom, and this aids in emotional expression and comprehension.

Mindfulness Within the Green

Many people prefer to practice their mindfulness techniques in the wonderful landscape that nature has to offer. This is mainly because nature has a way of grounding us. By engaging the mind during planting sessions and encouraging the children to focus on the sensory experience, like the coolness of the soil, tending to the soil, identifying seeds and plants, and the way the soil feels as they dig into the Earth, this practice will not only hold their attention but also instill a sense of calm and appreciation for the moment. It also gives them a sense of control over their fluctuating emotions and stress.

Social-Emotional Learning

Gardening and the dynamic interplay of growth and interaction will serve as fertile ground for social and emotional learning. This will not only equip the children with essential life skills but also help them develop empathy, teamwork, and self-awareness. A simple way of understanding this concept is to take the act of planting seeds as a metaphor for cultivating empathy. As the seeds begin to grow and sprout, speak about topics related to empathy. Refer to the growth of the plant as a metaphor. This way, the children will understand the parallels between nurturing plants and nurturing relationships. Also, have discussions and activities that are centered on emotions and cooperation. This will contribute to the growth of both the plants and their emotional intelligence.

Therapeutic Endeavors

Lastly, we get into therapy, where nature, along with its profound symbolism, is going to become a therapist in this well-rounded approach. Here, you'll be harnessing the power of storytelling through the language of the garden. So, speak about the growth cycle of plants in relation to resilience, change, and the interconnectedness of life. You can use the life cycle of plants as a metaphor for personal growth. For example, in the same way that seeds blossom into flowers, children can use these examples to draw parallels to their journey in life. This exploration will aid in their understanding of change and becoming mentally strong, especially in the face of challenges. Eventually, they'll discover the beauty of evolving and learning from their experiences.

The bottom line is that the garden can become a metaphorical haven where emotions are acknowledged, resilience is cultivated, and life's interconnected lessons can be learned. These techniques that we have already looked at contribute to the flourishing of not just the plants that you will be growing but the emotional landscapes of the children involved in the program as well. But now, you may ask the question: Do I need some specific place to practice gardening for my kids? Let's answer this now.

Nurturing Growth at Home

"Wait, pickles come from cucumbers?" my niece said when she made the connection.

Gardening doesn't need acres of land. Picture your backyard transformed into the canvas of growth that we have been referring to throughout the previous chapters. Here, flowers are going to bloom alongside your child's confidence, compassion, and empathy, which will accompany their emotional development. In this chapter, we are going to explore the magic that happens when the principles of gardening, counseling, mindfulness, and social-emotional learning come together in the intimate setting of your home.

Step-by-Step Guide on How to Garden at Home

Step 1: Observe Your Yard Space

- Look around for potential areas that can serve as a garden for your child to work in. If there is a small area, this is still okay, since you can come up with creative ideas for using small spaces.

- If the area is not garden-friendly, you can come up with planting trays or pots that you can use to plant and keep on windowsills, a balcony or patio. Anything can work out if you put your mind to it.

Step 2: Style and Grow

- You can tailor the area to suit your child's tastes. For example, use plants with the colors they love or use funny cutouts of their favorite animals to point out specific plants in the garden, like a green dinosaur for cabbage or an orange one for marigolds.

Step 3: Incorporate Therapy Into Gardening

- Use the tranquil environment to engage in open conversations with your child.

- Introduce mindfulness practices into your gardening routine. Pause and observe the intricate details of a blooming flower, listen to the soothing sounds of wind brushing through leaves, or simply breathe in the earthy fragrance of soil.

- Assign responsibilities, set achievable goals, and celebrate small victories together. As your child cares for their garden, they learn responsibility, patience, and the satisfaction of nurturing growth—a lesson that extends beyond the garden's boundaries.

- Discuss growth, resilience, and the beauty of transformation. This will help your child comprehend complex emotions through tangible, relatable symbols.

In this homebound garden, you're not just growing plants; you're cultivating a foundation for emotional well-being. As we conclude this chapter, envision your home as a flourishing landscape where your child's emotional intelligence blossoms with every petal and leaf.

Chapter 9:

Gardening and Diversity, Equity, and Inclusion (DEI)

Gardening is for everyone. After all, we all need some green in our lives. So, let's explore the enriching connection between gardening and the principles of DEI, uncovering how the therapeutic benefits of gardening extend their roots to embrace everyone, irrespective of age, ability, or status. This is not an exaggeration; after all, my garden is my happy place.

Gardening as an Inclusive Therapeutic Tool

We have gone over the benefits of gardening as a form of therapy, but let's look at what it can offer individuals across different spectrums. It doesn't matter how old or who you are; getting your hands in the soil can serve as an effective therapeutic tool for anyone. Let's get into what it can do for you.

The Benefits

Whether you are digging the soil, sowing seeds, tending to the plants, arranging flowers, or sitting outdoors and immersing yourself in the natural environment, you can access the therapeutic refuge nature offers, providing a balm to soothe your worries and fears.

Let's not overlook the effects of digging, planting, weeding, and harvesting. Your body gets its daily dose of exercise; and guess what? The most attractive part here is that it's universally accessible as a form of exercise that transcends ability, age, and background.

Along with a physical workout, when we plan a garden setup, identify plants, and understand and learn about key routines, we'll be engaging our minds. This will stimulate cognitive function as well as promote mental well-being, regardless of your age or background.

The benefits are endless, from cognitive and sensory stimulation to a source of inspiration, creativity, motivation, and a way to bring people together thus strengthening social bonds. This isn't an activity that's just about plants; it's a powerhouse that has tangible benefits for both your mental and emotional well-being. You get to trigger a physical connection with nature as you dig in the ground and tend to the plants, which has quite an impact on elevating your mood. But it goes even further than the physiological effects, as it provides you with a structured and purposeful activity. It will instill in you a sense of accomplishment and pride as you witness the growth of your plants.

These are a few pictures my grandkids drew of us in the garden.

The process of tending and caring for a garden is a mindful practice that promotes relaxation and reduces symptoms of stress and anxiety. It is a practical and accessible activity that connects you with nature. It offers a holistic approach to enhancing your mental, physical, and emotional well-being. In the kaleidoscope of therapeutic benefits that gardening offers, it goes beyond cultivating plants; it nurtures a sense of belonging and well-being for all.

Here are my grandchildren picking tomatoes from my raised beds, also beautifully as previously pictured. The wooden flag in the raised bed is one of the many garden signs my children made many years ago.

As we conclude this chapter, we celebrate the diverse garden of therapeutic benefits. Gardening, with its inclusive essence, beckons individuals from all walks of life to partake in the beauty of growth, connection, and personal triumph. In the upcoming chapter, we will delve into the vital aspect of keeping up with therapeutic gardening despite changing weather.

Chapter 10:

Year-Round Gardening

In the rhythmic dance of the seasons, can a therapeutic garden become a year-round haven for growth, exploration, and learning? How do we keep the gardening spirit alive during the winter months? Fear not; seasonal issues can be overcome with a few creative approaches that sustain the green heartbeat of the garden in every season.

Cultivating Knowledge in Every Season

When autumn approaches, we already expect our gardens to lose their green and submit to the cold and dry months. But what if there was a way for you to work your way around the seasons? Below are a few ideas you could try out:

Indoor Gardening

Transform a room into a lush oasis by introducing indoor gardening setups. Select plants like herbs, succulents, or low-light varieties to thrive in the cozy confines of your indoor garden. * If you have any pets, always research to make sure plants are pet-friendly before bringing them indoors.

This is a few co-workers and I, enjoying a group painting class. We got to bring our sunflowers indoors.

Selecting Seasonal Plants

Embrace the winter chill with seasonal projects, such as growing cold-hardy crops like lettuce and kale. Engage children in experiments with bulbs, sprouting seeds, or propagating plants for a hands-on winter gardening experience.

Alternative Gardening Methods

Dive into the world of hydroponics or aeroponics. Foster scientific inquiry by enabling children to monitor nutrient levels, pH, and plant growth in soil-less systems.

Gardening-Related Arts and Crafts

Infuse creativity by blending art and gardening. From crafting garden markers to constructing flower presses, these activities nurture fine motor skills and an appreciation for nature's aesthetic.

A great example of this can be seen below, where some friends and I are loving the opportunity to make a festive centerpiece out of dried flowers from a local nursery.

This is a mural a couple of students and I painted, bringing some nature indoors. We also use this tree to measure our student's growth over time.

Research

Ignite curiosity during the winter by encouraging children to dive into gardening-related research. Explore topics like plant adaptations to cold climates, the history of winter gardening, or the influence of light and temperature on plant growth.

As winter casts its enchanting spell, the garden becomes an ever-evolving area of learning and growth. By embracing these diverse approaches, you can weave a continuous thread of gardening experiences throughout the year, fostering skills, curiosity, and an enduring connection with nature in every child.

Conclusion

Nurturing growth through nature's classroom, where seeds of knowledge blossom into vibrant blooms, the journey through the pages of this book has unfolded the transformative power of gardening. From the delicate touch of a seed to the flourishing gardens within the heart and mind, we've explored how nature's embrace can catalyze the growth of children facing unique challenges.

As we close this chapter, let the roots of inspiration delve deep, for gardening is not merely a cultivation of plants but a nurturing of potential, resilience, and well-being. From sensory exploration to cognitive development, emotional regulation to social connections, the garden becomes a holistic sanctuary for young hearts and minds.

Yet, our exploration doesn't end here. The final bloom is just the beginning of a garden that extends beyond the classroom into homes, communities, and the hearts of all who come to understand the extraordinary impact of nature-based learning. As you embark on your journey to sow the seeds of growth, remember that each act of gardening is a testament to the profound belief that every child, regardless of challenges, deserves to flourish.

So, let the gardening spirit thrive, and may the knowledge shared within these pages inspire you—educators, parents, and caregivers—to create spaces where children can blossom into resilient, confident, and compassionate individuals. As we part ways, let the rhythm of growth echo in the wind, whispering tales of the gardens we nurture and the futures we cultivate.

May your gardens be abundant, your hearts be open, and your impact be everlasting. Happy gardening!

References

Ainamani, H. E., Gumisiriza, N., Bamwerinde, W. M., & Rukundo, G. Z. (2022). Gardening activity and its relationship to mental health: Understudied and untapped in low-and middle-income countries. *Preventive Medicine Reports, 29*, 101946. https://doi.org/10.1016/j.pmedr.2022.101946

Barnett, T. (2021, November 8). *Therapeutic Gardening For Kids - How Gardening Helps Kids With Behavioral Problems.* Gardening Know How. https://www.gardeningknowhow.com/special/children/behavioral-problems-and-gardening.htm#:~:text=Therapeutic%20gardening%20for%20kids%20is

Kohlmeyer, S. (2006). *Therapy Gardens Healing Environments for Children Therapy Gardens Healing Environments for Children.* https://digitalcommons.usu.edu/cgi/viewcontent.cgi?article=1763&context=honors

Pollin, S., & Retzlaff-Fürst, C. (2021, April 22). *The School Garden: A Social and Emotional Place.* Frontiers. https://www.frontiersin.org/articles/10.3389/fpsyg.2021.567720/full

Robbins, J. (2020, January 9). *Ecopsychology: How Immersion in Nature Benefits Your Health.* Yale E360. https://e360.yale.edu/features/ecopsychology-how-immersion-in-nature-benefits-your-health#:~:text=These%20studies%20have%20shown%20that

Dedication

I would like to thank a few special people who have inspired me to write this book and continue with my ambitions. Thank you, Jack, for being an inspiration. My family and friends, especially my husband and parents—my biggest fans! Their unwavering support serves as nourishment, encouraging my growth. My children and grandchildren... my heart blossoms with gratitude for the growth, love, and joy they bring to my garden of life. I am also forever grateful for loved ones who have passed. Your presence lingers, rooted deep within my heart, forever cherished in my garden of memories.

For the literally hundreds of students I've worked with over the last 26 years... Watching you all "bloom" has kept me young and makes me smile every day!

A Couple of Takeaways

Here is some advice for new therapists or anyone working with children, especially in special education:

- Before putting work in front of them, get to know your students first!

- Play with them! Get on the floor, dig in the dirt and interact with them. Ask them about their interests, about their family or whoever is in their lives, their pets, games they like, and so on.

- I see so many new therapists and educators who want to jump right in and address the education plan without taking the time to actually get to know the person behind that document. Reading a very well-written plan with a descriptive paragraph about a student won't compare to the connection you will make by first taking the time to get to know the child.

- If possible—and with all safety considerations in mind, of course—try doing this before you read through the pages and pages of reasons why they are in need of your help in the first place. This will give you a raw and untarnished opinion as you look at the person who's probably coming to you with a long list of diagnoses and baggage.

- Earn their trust, and you will be rewarded with a much more meaningful and productive therapeutic experience.

It doesn't have to be gardening. Use whatever method that you and your student, client, patient, parent, child, whoever, show interest in. Another passion of mine is woodworking! Stay tuned, because that just might be the theme of my next book!

www.ingramcontent.com/pod-product-compliance
Lightning Source LLC
Chambersburg PA
CBHW080849120626
46553CB00009B/2630